Have Fun with Arts and Crafts

Pirates

Rita Storey

A+

Smart Apple Media

Published by Smart Apple Media, an imprint of Black Rabbit Books
P.O. Box 3263, Mankato, Minnesota 56002
www.blackrabbitbooks.com

Published by arrangement with the Watts Publishing Group LTD, London.

Library of Congress Cataloging-in-Publication Data

Storey, Rita.
Pirates / by Rita Storey.
pages cm.—(Have fun with arts and crafts)
Includes index.
Summary: "Provides step by step instructions to create pirate-
themed crafts from everyday household objects. Easy-to-
follow directions for a pirate hat, compass, spyglass, and
more are included. Also features a recipe for hardtack
biscuits and instructions to make and play a board
game"—Provided by publisher.
ISBN 978-1-59920-900-5 (library binding)
1. Handicraft—Juvenile literature.
2. Pirates—Juvenile literature. I. Title.
TT157.S8258 2014
745.5--dc23
                                  2012042905

Series editor: Amy Stephenson
Packaged for Franklin Watts by Storeybooks
rita@storeybooks.co.uk
Designer: Rita Storey
Editor: Nicola Barber
Crafts: Rita Storey
Photography: Tudor Photography, Banbury
www.tudorphotography.co.uk

Cover images Shutterstock (top left), Tudor Photography, Banbury

Before You Start

Some of the projects in this book require scissors, paint, glue, a sewing needle, or an oven.
When using these things, we recommend that children are supervised by a responsible adult.

Printed in the United States of America
at Corporate Graphics, North Mankato, Minnesota
PO1588
2-2013

9 8 7 6 5 4 3 2 1

Contents

Captain Jack's Pirate Hat

Ahoy there! Come aboard our pirate ship and make a tricorne (three-cornered hat) to wear. This hat is like the one worn by Captain Jack Sparrow in *Pirates of the Caribbean*.

To make a swashbuckling captain's hat, you will need

- strong, brown paper 20 inches (50 cm) square
- pencil
- string about 12 inches (30 cm) long
- masking tape
- scissors
- strong, brown paper 16 inches (40 cm) square
- mixing bowl 12 inches (20 cm) across
- glue
- dark brown paint and large paintbrush
- 3 pins
- needle and embroidery thread

1 Crumple the large piece of brown paper into a ball. Flatten it out again. Fold it in half and then into quarters.

2 Tie the pencil to the string. Cut the string to the length of one side of the paper. Tape the other end of the string to the corner of the paper where all the folds meet.

3 Holding the string tight, draw a quarter circle on the paper from corner to corner.

4 Shorten the string to 3½ inches (9 cm) long and draw a second quarter circle. Carefully remove the tape. Cut along the pencil lines. Open the paper. This will be the brim of the hat.

5 Repeat steps 1–3 with the smaller piece of brown paper. Cut out along the pencil lines.

6 Turn the bowl upside down. To make the crown of the hat, squash the smaller circle of paper over the upturned bowl. Put strips of masking tape around the crown ¾ inch (2 cm) from the bottom edge of the bowl. Remove the paper hat from the bowl. Trim the edges.

7 Drop the brim of the hat over the crown. Use four small pieces of masking tape to lightly tape the brim to the crown.

8 Turn the hat over and rest the crown in the bowl. Make small cuts in the tape, about 1½ inches (2 cm) apart, down to where it meets the brim.

9 Take the hat out of the bowl and turn it over. Carefully peel off the four pieces of masking tape and remove the brim. Bend the flaps out. Spread glue on the flaps.

10 Drop the brim down over the crown and press it on to the flaps. Allow it to dry.

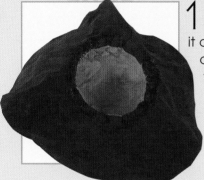

11 Paint the hat and let it dry. Turn the hat over and paint the underside of the brim. Allow it to dry.

12 To create a tricorne shape, fold the brim of the hat up to the crown in three places, equally spaced around the crown. Pin the edges of the brim together where they come to a point. Thread the needle with a length of embroidery thread and tie a knot in the end. Push the needle through the brim where it is pinned. Make two stitches at right angles to each other to make a cross. Knot the end of the thread at the back. Repeat by the other two pins. Remove the pins.

Aye, aye, Captain!

"Eye-spy" Spyglass

Pirates were always on the lookout for ships to plunder. You too can scan the horizon with this spyglass. It's easy to make and moves just like the real thing.

To make a super spyglass, you will need

- two tubes, one slightly smaller in diameter than the other
- scissors
- cling wrap and rubber band
- wrapping paper
- clear tape
- colored paper
- glue

1 Make small cuts about ¼ inch (5 mm) long and ¼ inch (5 mm) apart in the end of the larger cardboard tube to make flaps.

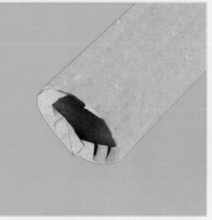

2 Bend the flaps in toward the inside of the tube.

3 Tightly stretch a piece of cling wrap across the other end. Secure with a rubber band.

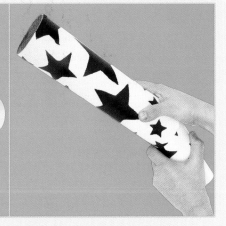

4 Cut a piece of wrapping paper to cover each tube. Each piece should be the same length as a tube and wide enough to wrap around it.

5 Secure the paper with clear tape.

6 Push the small tube into the end of the large one. The small tube should slide in and out of the large tube just like a real spyglass. The flaps will hold the small tube in place.

7 Cut strips of colored paper long enough to wrap around the tubes. Glue them in place around the ends of the tubes.

Put the end of the small tube up to your eye and keep a watch for enemy ships on the horizon.

Ship ahoy on the starboard side, Captain!

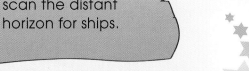

Spyglass

A spyglass is a type of small telescope that can be collapsed and carried around in a pocket. Pirates used spyglasses to scan the distant horizon for ships.

Pirate Outfit

A pirate lad or lass only had one set of clothes—the ones they were wearing. Find some old clothes, and add these pirate accessories to make a swashbuckling pirate outfit.

To make a fearsome cutlass and a silver buckle, you will need

- felt-tip pen • sheet of thin cardstock
- scissors • masking tape • poster board
- silver paint • paintbrush

For an eyepatch, you will need

- black felt • scissors • thin ribbon

To finish off your pirate outfit, you will need

- white or striped T-shirt
- pair of black or brown pants
- boots • long scarf
- red headscarf
- kerchief

Cutlass

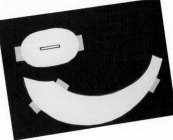

1 Copy the template for the cutlass blade and hand guard on page 30–31 onto the cardstock.

2 Tape the shapes to the poster board with masking tape. Draw around the shapes. Cut them out. Cut out the slit in the handle.

3 Paint both sides with silver paint. Allow it to dry.

4 Slide the slit in the hand guard down over the blade as far as it will go.

Buckle

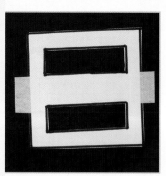

1 Follow steps 1–2 above. But this time, copy and cut out the buckle shape.

2 Paint the buckle silver. Allow it to dry.

Eyepatch

1 Cut a triangle of felt 4½ in x 2¾ in (12 cm x 7 cm).

2 Round off the corners. Cut a small slit in both sides of the eyepatch as shown.

3 Cut a piece of ribbon long enough to go around your head plus enough length to tie at the back. Thread the ribbon through the holes.

Pirate Outfit

1 Put on the T-shirt and pants. Tuck the pants into the boots. Thread the long scarf through the buckle and tie it around your waist.

2 Tie a red scarf around your head. Tie a kerchief around your neck. Tie on your eyepatch and wear your tricorne hat (see pages 4–5). Brandish your cutlass—you are ready to be a real pirate!

Hardtack Cookies

These yummy cookies are a lot nicer than the biscuits pirates used to eat on their long voyages. Ship's biscuits were so hard that pirates often broke their teeth on them. Pirates called them "hardtack."

To make pirate cookies, you will need

- 2 cups (250 g) plain flour
- 1 teaspoon (5 mL) baking powder
- ½ cup (120 mL) margarine or butter
- ⅓ cup (115 g) superfine sugar
- 1 egg
- 1 teaspoon (5 mL) vanilla flavoring
- red and pink fondant icing
- tube of black writing icing
- bowl
- wooden spoon
- sifter
- rolling pin
- 2¼ inch (6 cm) biscuit cutter
- baking sheet
- wire rack

Before you start, have an adult set the oven to 350°F (180°C).

1 Put the flour, baking powder, butter, and sugar into a bowl.

2 Mix it together with your fingers (clean hands, please!) until the mixture does not have any big lumps in it.

3 Add the egg and vanilla flavoring.

4 Mix with the wooden spoon. Keep mixing until the mixture sticks together. Then use your hands to make the mixture into a ball of dough.

5 Sift some flour on to a work surface.

6 Roll out the dough so that it is about ⅛ inch (3 mm) thick.

7 Use the biscuit cutter to cut out 12 circles.

8 Put the cookies on a greased baking sheet. Ask an adult to put the baking sheet into the preheated oven. Cook for 15 minutes.

9 Ask an adult to take the cookies out of the oven. Put the cookies on a wire rack to cool. Don't forget to turn off the oven!

10 When the cookies are cool, roll out the red and pink fondant icing thinly. Cut out circles using the biscuit cutter.

11 Cut the circles in half and press a red semicircle and a pink semicircle on to each cookie.

12 Use the black writing icing to draw on an eyepatch, an eye, a mouth, and a nose. Add dots of black icing to the hat.

Make lots of cookies as snacks for your pirate crew.

Pirate Treasure Chest

Pirates buried their treasure in strong treasure chests to hide it from other pirates. Hide all your special loot in this chest.

To make a treasure chest, you will need

- shoe box with lid
- ruler
- pencil
- thin cardstock
- compass
- scissors
- glue
- brown paint
- stiff brush
- gold tape or strips of gold cardstock
- paper
- gold cardstock
- clear tape

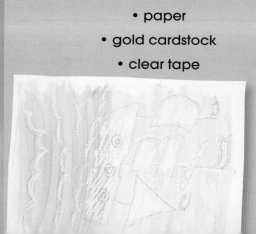

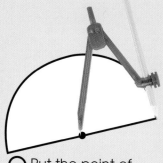

1 Measure the short side of the shoe box. Draw a line the same length on the thin cardstock. Measure half way across the line and draw a dot.

2 Put the point of the compass on the dot. Open the compass so the pencil is at the end of the line. Draw a semicircle. Keeping the point of the compass in the same place, open the compass out another ½ inch (1 cm). Draw a second semicircle outside the first.

3 Cut out the cardstock along the line of the larger semicircle.

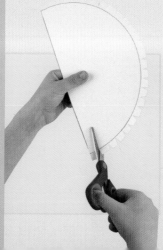

4 Cut small V-shapes from the outside of the semicircle up to the first line at ½ inch (1 cm) intervals to make tabs. Repeat steps 1–3 to make another semicircle.

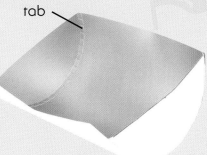

tab

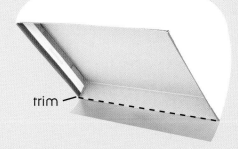

trim

5 To make the top of the treasure chest, cut a piece of cardstock the same size as the long side of the box lid and twice the length of the short side.

6 Fold back the tabs around one of the semicircles. Glue the long piece of cardstock to the tabs. Repeat with the second semicircle keeping the tabs on the inside of the curved shape.

7 The lid of the shoe box should fit inside the shape. Place it inside the shape and tape the straight sides of the shape on to the top of the lid of the shoe box. Trim off any cardstock that overlaps.

8 Paint the box with the brown paint. Use the stiff brush to make patterns in the paint to look like wood. Allow it to dry. Trim the edges of the lid and base with gold tape or strips of gold cardstock.

9 Use the templates on page 31 to trace two handles, a catch, and a lock on to paper. Cut them out. Draw around them onto gold cardstock. Glue them on to the front and sides of the box. Fill the box with all your special treasures.

Keep your treasure safe from other pirates.

Treasure Map Game

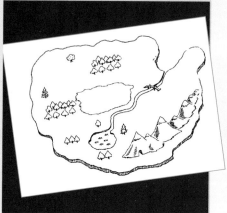

Ahoy there, mateys! Challenge your motley crew to a swashbucklin' adventure. Not for the lily-livered, this pirate voyage is full of dangers. Beware—not everyone will make it to claim the buried treasure.

To make a treasure map game, you will need

- 8½ inch x 11 inch (21 cm x 30 cm) sheet of cardstock
- pencil, felt-tip pens, paints, crayons
- ruler
- large piece of colored paper 12 ½ inches x 9 inches (32 cm x 23 cm)
- large piece of poster board or thick cardstock 12 ½ inches x 9 inches (32 cm x 23 cm)
- glue
- scraps of thick cardstock
- scissors
- one die

1 Draw an island shape on the smaller piece of cardstock. Draw trees, rivers, and mountains on the island.

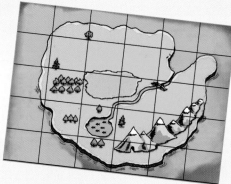

2 Color or paint the island and the water around it. Draw lines to divide the map into 30 squares.

3 Glue the map onto a larger piece of colored paper. Glue the colored paper onto poster board or thick cardstock. Number the squares from the bottom left to the top right starting at 1. Write "Set sail" in square 1 and "You win!" in square 30. Draw a treasure chest on square 21.

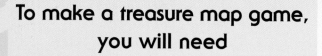

4 Think of some things that could happen along the way to stop the pirates from getting to their treasure. Write an instruction for what to do if you land on these squares.

5 You can use real coins for the playing pieces, or you can make your own. Cut circles small enough to fit on the squares of the board from scraps of poster board or thick cardstock. Paint or color them to look like old coins.

How to play the game

Each player has a counter and puts it on square 1 ("Set sail").
The first player rolls the die.
Move the counter the number of squares shown on the die.
If there is an instruction on the square, do as it says.
Take turns rolling the die.
The winner is the first one to reach the treasure and escape with it to square 30. When you get close to the square containing the treasure chest, you must roll the exact number to land on it.

Aye, there be plenty of doubloons for them that get there first.

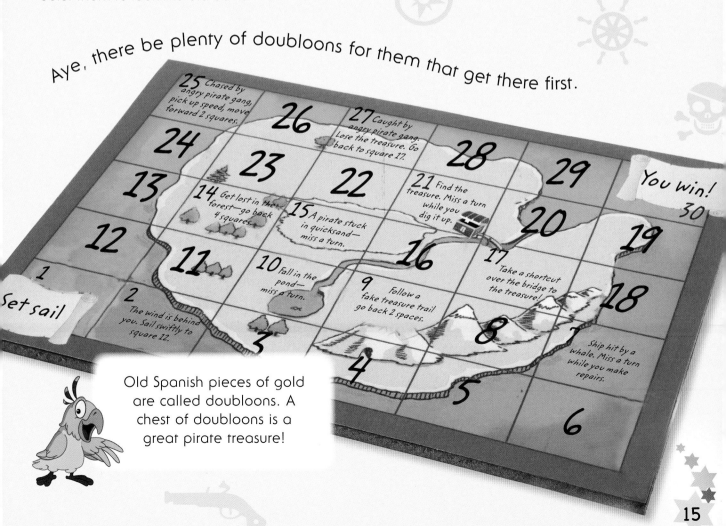

Old Spanish pieces of gold are called doubloons. A chest of doubloons is a great pirate treasure!

Deep-sea Octopus

Pirates are always on the lookout for deadly sea monsters. This octopus, with its eight arms, is lurking and ready to attack. It will eat any pirates that fall overboard as a tasty snack.

To make this crazy creature, you will need

- 4 pairs of thick, clean tights
- scissors
- pillow stuffing
- 10 strong rubber bands
- needle and strong thread
- felt in black, white, and some bright colors
- fabric glue

1 Cut the legs off the tights near to the body.

2 Stuff the legs with the stuffing to within about 4 inches (10 cm) of the top. Fasten the top of each one with a small rubber band.

3 Gather the top of all the legs together near the rubber bands. Use another rubber band to secure the legs. Twist the rubber band several times until it is tight.

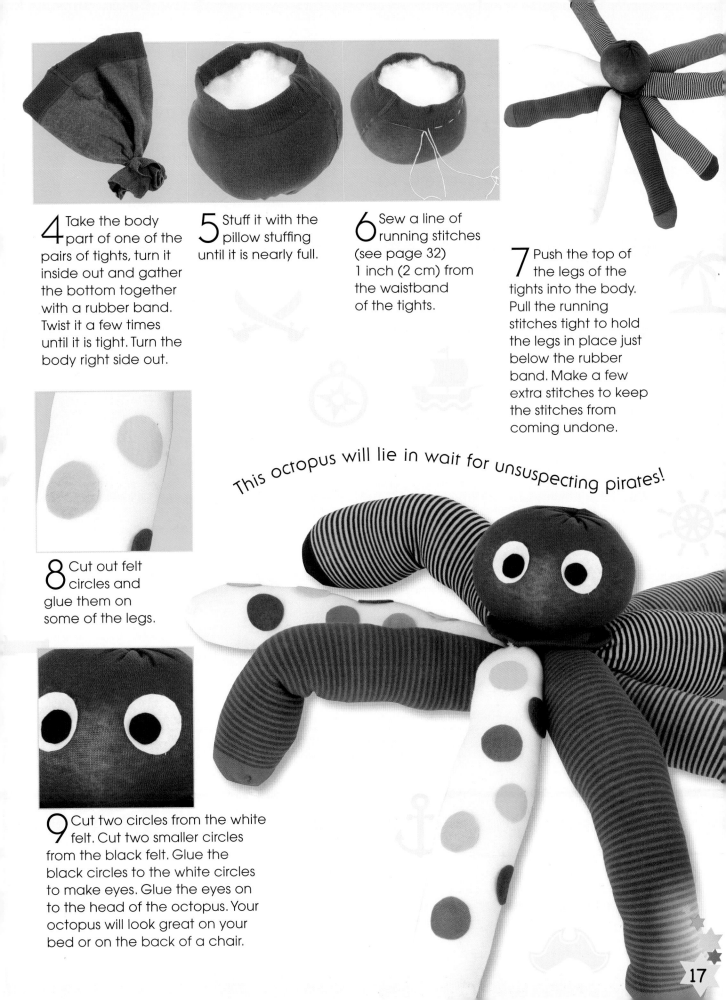

4 Take the body part of one of the pairs of tights, turn it inside out and gather the bottom together with a rubber band. Twist it a few times until it is tight. Turn the body right side out.

5 Stuff it with the pillow stuffing until it is nearly full.

6 Sew a line of running stitches (see page 32) 1 inch (2 cm) from the waistband of the tights.

7 Push the top of the legs of the tights into the body. Pull the running stitches tight to hold the legs in place just below the rubber band. Make a few extra stitches to keep the stitches from coming undone.

This octopus will lie in wait for unsuspecting pirates!

8 Cut out felt circles and glue them on some of the legs.

9 Cut two circles from the white felt. Cut two smaller circles from the black felt. Glue the black circles to the white circles to make eyes. Glue the eyes on to the head of the octopus. Your octopus will look great on your bed or on the back of a chair.

A Motley Crew

Pirate captains used to round up any sailors they could find to make up their crews. See what you can find to create your own pirate crew of finger puppets.

To make a basic finger puppet, you will need

- piece of paper • felt-tip pen
- scissors • felt • pin
- needle and thread

To make a pirate's parrot, you will need

- basic finger puppet made from green felt
- glue • googly eyes
- scrap of yellow felt • scissors • feathers

To make a pirate puppet, you will need

- basic finger puppet made from blue felt
- styrofoam ball
- pink paint • paintbrush
- lollipop stick • modeling clay
- felt-tip pen • red paint • glue
- scraps of blue, pink, and brown felt
- scissors • gold and silver paper

Basic Finger Puppet

1 Draw around your finger on the paper. Leave a ½ inch (1 cm) gap all the way around. Cut out the shape.

2 Put two pieces of felt on top of each other. Pin the template to the felt. Cut out the shape.

3 Sew the two pieces together ¼ inch (5 mm) from the edge, using a backstitch (see page 32). Do not stitch across the straight edge. Trim off the excess fabric.

4 Turn the shape inside out and press flat under a book.

Pirate's Parrot

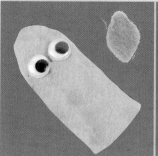

1 Glue the googly eyes on the green finger puppet. Cut out a diamond shape for the beak. Pinch it together at one corner and glue it on the finger puppet just below the eyes.

2 Glue feathers on the top of the parrot at the back to make plumage. Glue feathers on each side to make wings.

Pirate Puppet

1 Push one end of the lollipop stick into the styrofoam ball and the other end into the clay. Stick the clay onto a work surface. Paint the styrofoam ball pink. Allow it to dry.

2 Use a felt-tip pen to draw on an eye, an eyebrow, a moustache, and an eyepatch. Paint a red hat. Allow it to dry.

3 Take the styrofoam ball off the lollipop stick. Press the top of the felt finger puppet down to make a little dent. Glue the bottom of the head into the dent in the felt.

4 Using the templates on page 30, cut out two arms from blue felt and two hands from pink felt. Glue one arm on each side of the finger puppet's body.

7 Glue on a tiny felt beard. Cut out a cutlass (sword) from silver paper and glue it on one hand. Use your puppets to act out a pirate story about your pirate and his parrot friend.

5 Glue a hand to the bottom of each arm.

6 To make a belt, cut a strip of brown felt long enough to go around the puppet. Glue it around the bottom of the finger puppet. Cut a square of gold paper. Color a square in the center. Glue it on to the belt to make a buckle.

A Ghostly Pirate Ship

There have been lots of sightings of ghost ships over the years. Make this fantastic ghost pirate ship picture to hang on your wall. The wax picture will appear through the paint like a ghostly pirate ship appearing through the sea mist.

To make this ghostly ship, you will need

- 11 in. x 17 in. (29 cm x 42 cm) sheet of white paper
- masking tape
- blue, red, and yellow crayons
- white candle
- watercolor paints
- big paintbrush
- piece of cardstock 15 ½ in. x 17 in. (40 cm x 44 cm)

1 Tape the paper onto a work surface with the masking tape. Use the blue crayon to draw a picture of a pirate ship and lots of waves on the paper. Draw a moon with the yellow crayon. Draw portholes and flags with the red crayon.

2 Draw over the outline again with the unlit candle. Fill in the sails and boat with the candle. Add some waves and swirling mist. Do not worry if you cannot see the candle wax—it will show on the finished picture.

3 Mix the watercolor paints with water to make runny sea colors.

4 Swish the paint across the whole paper with the big brush.

5 The paint colors the paper, but it will not stick to the wax, so the wax outline stays white. Allow the picture to dry.

6 Carefully peel off the masking tape. Glue the picture to a piece of cardstock.

The *Flying Dutchman*

The film *Pirates of the Caribbean* features the *Flying Dutchman*, a phantom ship doomed to roam the seas. This ship is based on an old legend. According to the story, the captain of the *Flying Dutchman* was cursed never to sail into port, but to haunt the oceans forever. Sailors believed that it was bad luck to catch a glimpse of this ghostly ship.

The Captain's Parrot

Pirates were often at sea for months on end. For company, some kept parrots as pets. You can make yourself a feathery friend to take on your next voyage.

To make a captain's parrot, you will need

- 8½ inch x 11 inch (21 cm x 30 cm) sheet of yellow paper
- 8½ inch x 6 inch (22 cm x 15 cm) sheet of green paper
- 8½ inch x 6 inch (22 cm x 15 cm) sheets of colored paper
  - felt-tip pen
  - scissors
  - pipe cleaner
  - 2 googly eyes
  - glue
  - craft feathers
  - string
  - tape

1 Copy the parrot template on page 30 onto a sheet of colored paper. Cut it out.

2 Glue the small circle to the top of the oval shape.

3 Bend the pipe cleaner in half. Bend the ends to make a loop on each end. Bend each end again to make a second loop. Glue the middle of the legs to the back of the oval at the bottom.

4 Fold the triangle of paper in half. Open it out.

5 Fold back a small flap on each side.

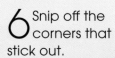

6 Snip off the corners that stick out.

7 Glue the small flaps on the beak in the middle of the head, so the beak sticks out. Glue on two googly eyes.

8 Fold a piece of 8½ in. x 6 in. (22 cm x 15 cm) colored paper in half.

9 Draw the shape of half a feather and cut it out.

10 Make cuts along the unfolded edges of the feather, stopping ½ inch (1 cm) from the fold.

11 Make two more feathers. Glue them to the back of the parrot behind the feet to make a tail. Glue the craft feathers on each side of the parrot to make wings. Glue a feather to the top of the head to make plumage. Glue feathers on the body of the parrot.

12 Attach a loop of string to the back of the head of the parrot with tape. Hang up your colorful parrot.

"Pieces of eight!"

Long John Silver is the one-legged pirate in the book *Treasure Island*. He named his parrot Captain Flint. The parrot sat on Long John Silver's shoulder and was often heard to shriek, "Pieces of eight! Pieces of eight!" In fact, pieces of eight were silver coins.

"Pieces of eight! Pieces of eight!"

Into the Deep

Davy Jones's locker is where dead pirates end up—at the bottom of the sea. It is a place full of strange plants and sea creatures. Make this magical underwater scene and fill it with imaginary creatures.

For your underwater scene, you will need

- paper
- masking tape
- blue and green paints
- brushes
- bubble wrap
- colored ink
- drinking straw
- aluminum foil
- scissors
- glue
- colored paper
- foam
- yarn or ribbon
- googly eyes
- glitter glue

1 Tape a sheet of paper to a work surface with masking tape. Add water to a blob of blue paint until it is very runny. Paint a watery background on the paper. Let it dry.

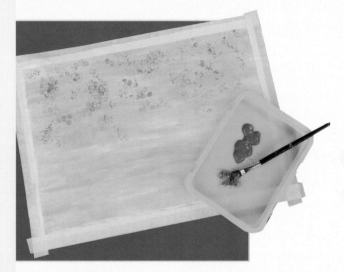

2 Cut some pieces of bubble wrap. Paint the bumpy side of the bubbles. Use the painted side to stamp bubbles on the paper.

3 Drip blobs of ink on the paper. Blow through the straw to make weird and wonderful underwater plants.

4 Cut sparkly fish from aluminum foil. Glue them on to the picture.

5 Cut out some fish shapes from the colored paper and glue them on to the picture.

6 Cut the top of a jellyfish out of the foam. Cut lengths of yarn or ribbon and glue these below the jellyfish body. Add googly eyes and decorate with glitter glue.

7 Cut out a star fish from colored paper. Glue it on to the picture, and decorate with glitter glue.

No one knows all the creatures at the bottom of the sea. You can make up some new creatures of your own.

Meet some sparkly sea creatures in this watery deep-sea scene!

Shipwreck in the Ocean

When pirates were not busy plundering ships, they could spend their time making ships inside bottles. You can do one better—impress your crew with this shipwreck scene under rolling ocean waves.

1 Wash the bottle and remove the label. Using the funnel, pour the gravel or sand into the bottle.

To make this ocean shipwreck, you will need

- empty, clear plastic bottle with tight-fitting lid and a wide neck
- funnel
- handful of colorful gravel (used in fish tanks) or coarse sand
- a few shells
- small plastic toy ship
- water
- cooking oil or baby oil
- blue food coloring

2 Drop the shells and the plastic ship into the bottle.

3 Using the funnel, fill the bottle a quarter of the way up with water.

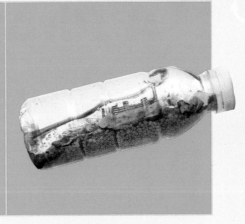

4 Using the funnel, add oil so the bottle is half full.

5 Add a few drops of blue food coloring. Ask an adult to put the lid on the bottle very tightly.

6 Turn the bottle on its side and rock it gently to see the waves break over the shipwreck. You could rest your bottle on top of a small pile of gravel to keep it from rolling away.

Pirate Shipwreck

In April 1717, the *Whydah Gally*, ship of the famous pirate "Black Sam" Bellamy, sank in a huge storm off Cape Cod on the coast of Massachusetts. The wreck was rediscovered by divers in 1984. Although the ship was thought to be loaded with gold, silver, and jewelry when it sank, none was found and divers are still searching for the loot.

To make sure that no water or oil can leak from the bottle, ask an adult to seal the cap with strong glue or a hot glue gun.

Best batten down the hatches—there be a mighty storm brewing!

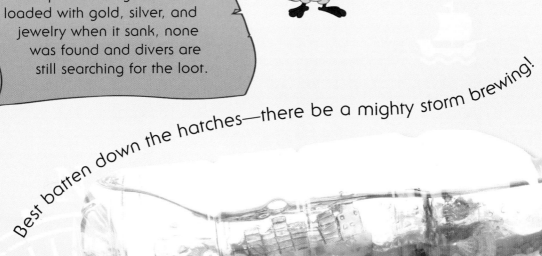

A Pirate Compass

Pirates need a good compass to navigate in the right direction. This handy compass will always tell you which way is north.

For a perfect pirate compass, you will need

- needle
- magnet
- pin
- paper
- felt-tip pen
- craft foam
- scissors
- tape or glue
- colored cardstock
- shallow cereal bowl
- small bowl
- gold and red paper
- glue
- paint
- clear tape
- jug of water

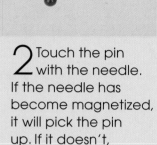

1 Holding the needle between your thumb and finger, stroke the magnet from the needle tip to the eye about 50 times.

2 Touch the pin with the needle. If the needle has become magnetized, it will pick the pin up. If it doesn't, repeat step 1.

3 Using the template on page 30, draw an arrow on the paper. Cut it out. Trace around this paper template on to the foam.

4 Cut out the shape. Attach the needle to the foam with a small piece of tape or a dot of glue.

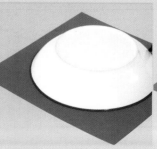

5 Draw around the cereal bowl on the cardstock. Cut ½ inch (1 cm) outside the ring you drew. Put the small bowl in the middle of the circle. Draw around it. Cut the inner circle out to make a ring.

6 To decorate the ring, cut triangle shapes from gold paper. Cut four diamond shapes from red paper.

7 Glue the triangles on the ring. Paint spots between the triangles. Glue diamonds equally spaced around the ring.

8 Write N, S, E, and W on the diamonds (see picture below for the correct order). Put the ring face down and place the cereal bowl on top. Tape the ring to the bowl.

9 Turn the bowl over. Carefully pour some water into the bowl, taking care not to spill any on the ring.

10 Gently place the foam arrow on the water with the needle on top. When the needle comes to rest, its pointed end will indicate north. Move the dish so that the arrow points to the N.

Weigh anchor, hoist the mizzen, and set a new course, me hearties!

The First Compass

The earliest compasses were made of lodestone, a type of magnetic rock. Pirates used compasses to help them navigate dangerous seas and to find hidden treasure.

Templates

Finger Puppet
Pages 18–19

Parrot
Pages 22–23

Arrow
Pages 28–29

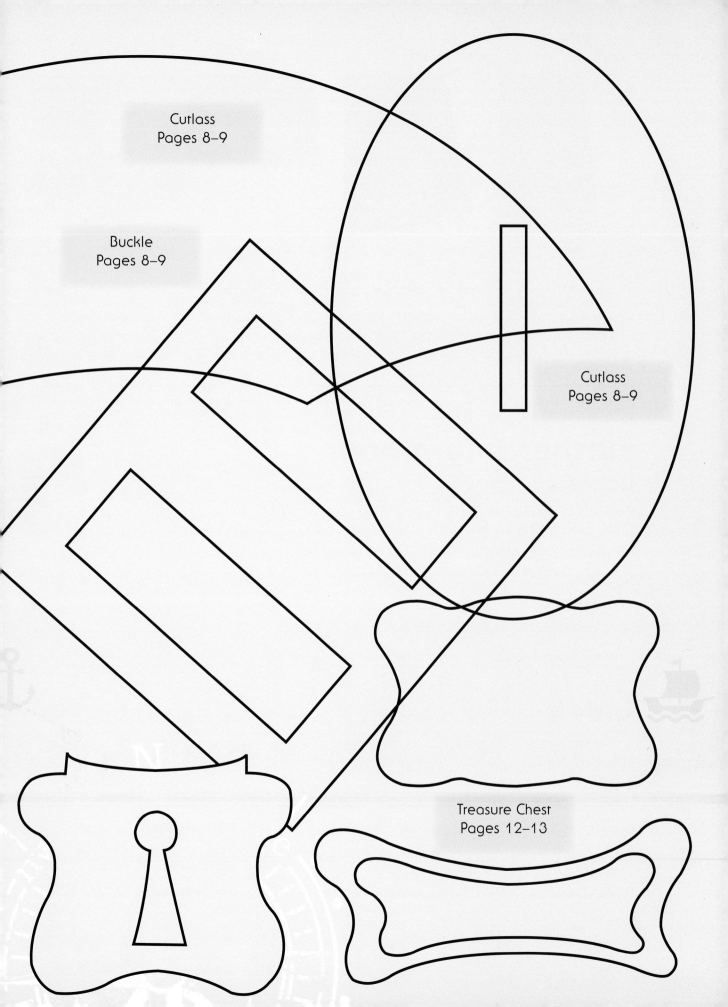

Cutlass
Pages 8–9

Buckle
Pages 8–9

Cutlass
Pages 8–9

Treasure Chest
Pages 12–13

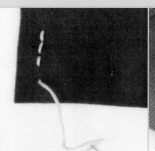
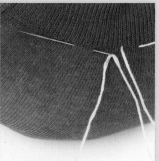

1 Tie a knot in the end of the thread. Push the needle up from the back of the fabric. Pull the thread through to the knot.

2 Push the needle down through the fabric just behind where it came up. Push the needle up from the back to just in front of the first stitch and pull it through.

3 Push the needle back down to join up with the last stitch. A row of backstitches will join up together.

1 Follow step 1 of the backstitch. Push the needle back down through the fabric in front of where it came up. Push the point of the needle up through the fabric just in front of where it went down. Pull the thread through. A row of running stitches will have gaps between the stitches.

Further Information

Books

Donaldson, Madeline. *Pirates, Scoundrels, and Scallywags (Villans).* Lerner Publications, 2013

Jenson-Elliott, Cynthia L. *The Most Famous Pirates (Blazers. Pirates!).* Capstone Press, 2013

Websites

www.nationalgeographic.com/pirates

Index